RANGOLI

pavana reddy

Rangoli
Copyright Pavana Reddy, 2017
All rights reserved

Design by Adam Peña & Tucker Neel
Drawings by Lakshmi Reddy
Cover photo by Paula Placido

Printed in the United States of America
ISBN–13: 978-1544961484
ISBN–10: 1544961480

For more information, or to order copies in bulk please visit
pavanareddy.com

in another life,
the storm isn't strong enough
to steal you away.

in another life,
we bloom.

dedicated to my sister

light a few candles
and burn a few bridges.
not everyone deserves
to be a part of your journey.

8

you can't forget
and call that healing.
one doesn't leap over the fire
and name that strength.

i am homesick
for a country
i know so well

a country
who no longer
knows me

brown is not a color.
it's a way of life
a way to struggle
a way to survive.

14

generations spent trying to reach home

we have survived
so many fires,
i can no longer tell
if we are alive
or simply burning.

children of immigrants
know the struggle
of being a book
opened to a random page
and told to understand

brown girl,
you are a poem
in a country
made entirely
of stories

22

the roots of my parents
grow from two different orchards,
their seeds have been planted within me

i was born outside
of both of their countries
and was left to grow roots of my own

for those of us whose bodies
are filled with foreign flowers
we long for the home that was cut out of the picture,
a phantom limb we can't stop touching,
and we spend our lives
marrying the seeds within us
so they may grow, as one,
in unfamiliar soil

some of us are flower gardens carrying no roots.
we sow our own earth
and water our own petals
to grow our own footing

we are left to create
beautiful orchards of our own
out of the two humble seeds
planted within our hearts.

melanin in my veins,
this heart pumps stars.

they said,

what an unfortunate mother
with a daughter so dark.

to them
my mother replied,

i'm so sorry
the sun did not
love you enough.

brown girl,
you are lovely
in every shade.

28

if only she knew
how beautiful her skin shone
beneath the light of the sun.
if only she saw the way
she blossomed,
a solitary lotus adrift upon
the stillness of the water,
she would understand
that some eyes
are murkier
than even the muddiest of rivers.

dark girl,
you wear
your pain
so beautifully.
you are a poem
just waiting
to be written.

to be a daughter
is to be a mistake,
a stain on a window
overlooking a beautiful sunrise.

there is no dawn
when you are the cloud
blurring out the sun.

brown girl, lower your gaze.
didn't anyone ever tell you that modesty
lies within the eye of the beholder?

brown girl, study harder, put the stories away.
what man would want to marry a girl
with a head so heavy with clouds?

brown girl, be quieter.
have you ever heard a flower bloom?

brown girl, stop giggling.
laughter is for shameless women.

brown girl, smile more.
haven't we given you everything
you've ever needed?

brown girl, stay out of the sun.
keep your mouth shut.
head down. fire smoldered.

brown girl, we pray you have a son.

brown girl is witchcraft
brown girl is wicked
brown girl holds the power to heal.

brown girl,
you are smoke from an incense stick.

brown girl
brown girl
you were always meant
to disappear.

you are not your roots.
you are a flower
grown from them.

38

i was born outside
of my mother's country.
for this,
i will always be
a foreigner.

40

they are afraid
of our brown,
of our light,
the resilience
of the earth
that is our skin.

they are afraid
because next to us
they know how foreign feels.

i am not
your exotic
country.

knowing me
does not
make you
a traveler.

44

my skin,

an eternal love affair
between the earth
and the sun.

a brown that blossoms.
a brown that holds.
a brown that burns.

46

you came to me
as a settler
wanting to unearth
my body
but you never
even bothered
to learn
my language.

48

i find myself always
struggling for breath
the way my name
drowns in your
ignorance.

50

it is not what the immigrant leaves behind,
but in the home
that is no longer spoken of.

a quiet heartbeat
slowly
continuing to fade.

54

even naked i am covered in stories.

56

culture has become
a bouquet of foreign flowers
decorating a dinner table.

no story of our roots,
only of how we were obtained.

58

how much
have we forgiven,
to forget.

how much more
have we forgotten,
to forgive?

forgetting is a privilege we have never been granted.

i still live on the edge
of nothingness,
between the east and
the west of who i am,
and who i want to be.

i still drink the fire of
the sun's mirage as it
settles into a distant sea,
but tread carefully so as
to not disturb the silence.

i still lie awake waiting
for a new dawn to arrive,
but she always forgets
to bring a new beginning.

64

when you ask me
where i'm from,
i cannot answer
without clearing my throat
of all the places
that have fallen in-between,

every home
that has tried
to make me forget.

66

foreigners
know the pain
of bending bones.

we are pillars
of memory,
spines shaped
by what has been forgiven,
but never forgotten.

you call me different
and it's true,
i was not made
with a single
forgiving bone
in my body.

i broke myself
to be alive.

this is what
forgiveness
looks like.

my mother smiles
through my poems,
asks me if i wrote this for her
and i answer yes, always.

and what about
your father,
where are his words?

she wants to know.

in ashes, i tell her,
like the memories of a home
i've long ago written about,
and forgotten

these words are yours now.
the thoughts you could never say
each flame you've ever swallowed,
manifested in me.

my poetry is but a silence
born of your own.

when there's nothing left to burn,
be the rain
who brings everything good
back to life.

74

silence as a body language.

76

my mother swallowed her voice
so when she spoke
others would listen.

but when she cries
i hear her native tongue.

when my mother cries,
i know how long she has been silent.

78

i was born tragedies ago,
a daughter of the fire
and of the rain,
i am as old as the sea.

my life did not begin
when i inhaled my first
breath of air,
for i am each struggled gasp
of my mother's ancestors.

i am generations of clay women
whose rain courses through me,

my birth is no celebration
when every passing year
is a miracle to still be alive.

your body is a burning city.
i wake up next to corpses
each time you let me in.

82

how pain
bellows
without sound

how bright
the glow of
a falling star

how quiet
its death.

within me
echoes the cries
of all the women
i set on fire
to become a woman
worth loving.

you will become a graveyard
of all the women you once were
before you rise one morning
embraced by your own skin.

you will swallow
a thousand different names
before you taste the meaning
held within your own.

speak less
my mother would say.

words are precious
and your life depends
on the amount we are each given.
keep them close to your heart
and write what you cannot speak,
for the pieces you share with this world
are the ones that will keep you a part of it
even after you are gone.

empty your words
into the margins of
this world

from what can no
longer be held,
a poem is born.

92

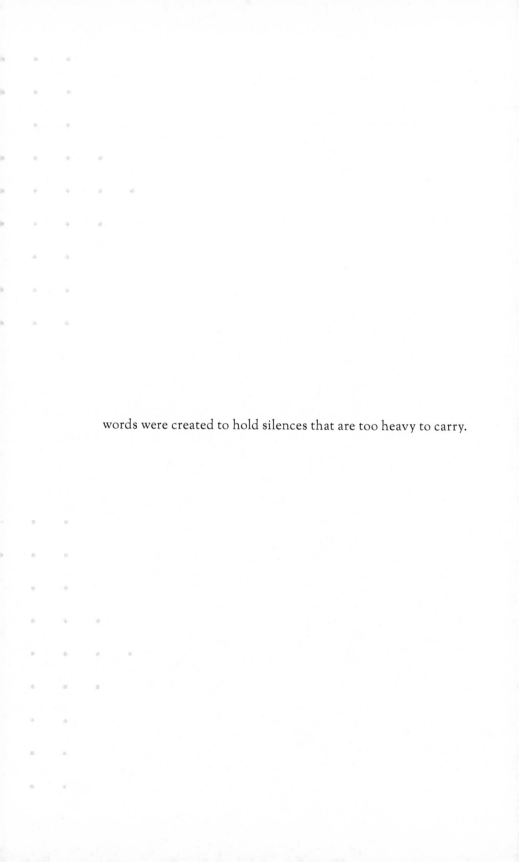

words were created to hold silences that are too heavy to carry.

i found so many words
after you left

had we stayed together
we may have become silence

96

there are some poems
that cannot be translated
for if they were,
the beauty held within
their native language
would be forever lost.

poets write for those
who will never
read their work,
it's a curse we carry
around with us
like the worn out luggage
our mothers carried
crossing the seas
separating them
from the only ones
who could ever understand.

the ocean sighs for the moon
in tidal waves, the trees
twist and shed their leaves
for their love of the wind,
the whole world stitches itself in poems.

we will never understand,
and this is why we write.

we write for the same reason
we keep secrets.

we write so that we may never
forget the language we no longer speak.

we build worlds
inside of our mouths
only to swallow them

we create homes
out of silences
and live there.

tell me the story about the quiet girl who smiled with her eyes
how for every year since she was sixteen lived inside a lotus garden.
tell me about the day she turned seventeen, how she gave all her petals
to a boy who slept on thorns and made love in bruises,
about the happiness her eyes made people believe in,
and how the dirt on her hands told a different story.

you swore you would never let this girl hurt again
you swore you would protect her,
so she unfolded herself for you,
petal by petal,
until she erased herself from your lips to write on your palms.

you both danced in the middle of winter
her hands on your shoulders as you threw back
your heads and laughed at the moon,
her lipstick blazing the sun's trail up and down your neck.
every story she told you reminded you of love,
love in the middle of innocence
love in the middle of a burning home.

you planted seeds in the garden she lived in
and slept beneath the fading stars
as she told you stories about the future,
about flowers that only grow after a fire,
how some are plucked before they have a chance to blossom
and how some blossom even after they are plucked.

tell me the story of the wilting girl you found
whose petals were covered in the filth from her own grave.
tell me how you helped her blossom anyway,
a lotus grown from the dirt.

countless are the number
of winters a writer will live
through before she can
write about spring.

104

i have silences
buried so deeply,
i weep when they blossom.

106

what language robbed
a woman's no from her lips
and left a man's yes in its place

108

speak to me in a language
no one else speaks,
a language that sings
in its mother's tongue,
which hasn't robbed
the voice
from between her lips
to leave a man's desire
in its place.

speak to me foreign,
as if my body
were a country
no one's ever heard of,

where the women
can scream
and still be heard.

my father was a storm
my mother,
the rain.

i was born from fire
but i inherited
the sea.

your mother
crashed her body
against the rocks
to give you
the calm of the sea.

you do not know pain
until it is your turn to carry
the weight of the storm
upon your tired back.

standing at the edge of our distances
the sun peeking far offshore

the sound of stretching water grows

116

how do we say goodbye in our language?
i asked my mother.

in oceans, she told me.
in the endless way she stretches.
this is how we say goodbye.

if you are a poet

i told my sister one night as we walked along the shore

if you really are a true magician of words
show me a trick. turn this pebble into a poem.

i watched her place the stone in the center of her palm
as she knelt down to pick up a tiny ant crawling along the sand.

look
she said
as the ant slowly climbed the pebble

to you this is merely a rock of little importance,
but to this ant
it is an entire lonely universe waiting to be discovered.

don't believe me yet?
let me show you another trick.

gently placing the ant
back in the sand,
in one fluid motion
i watched my sister
throw the pebble
into the lake

as it sunk beneath the ripples
she smiled at me.

see that?

what was once an entire universe
is nothing now but a grain of sand.

i asked my mother once,
where does the heart go
when it's ripped from
the motherland?

she handed me her own
and said,
wherever you carry it.

122

my mother calls to tell me about her day
and i listen, i know there's no one else who will.

my mother asks me to tell her about mine,
so i tell her only the good things and keep the rest inside
because words travel the distances her loving hands cannot.

my mother asks me if i am happy,
and i tell her that i am.

i ask her the same question and she says
yes, if you are, i am
and i know
that some lies are worth telling.

my mother reminds me to be strong through it all,
to remember to be modest
and to always keep my head up high.

i've given you everything,
she says, *make me proud.*

but my mother doesn't know that everything comes with
her shame attached,

that the child of an immigrant
cannot smile without guilt.
cannot feel without pain.
cannot be without fear.

my mother asks if i understand,
and i tell her yes, i can't unlearn it.

and when my mother asks when i'm coming home,
i know she's asking for me to never forget.

soon,
i promise her.
soon.

when was the last time someone ran their fingers through the knots of your soul?

128

tell me it isn't magic
the way you heal yourself

130

there is nothing
poetic
about my broken heart.

poetry is how
i put it back together.

show me your worst
the earth said to the storm,
and i will blossom anyway.

i've grown a meadow
inside of my heart
made entirely out of words

this is where i rest my tired bones.

i have written myself into peace,

for i have never been able to find any
outside of myself.

on some mornings
the loneliness inside my house
is so overwhelming,
i have to leave
and sit among the flowers
just to breathe.

it's on mornings like these
that i remember how beautiful
the world really is,
and how little has changed
since you've been gone.

i guess this is what letting go
really means,

it's feeling you everywhere
and still appreciating the world
for never letting go of me.

138

i don't know who i am,
but it's the only person
i know how to be.

140

touch
your wounds
with forgiveness.

142

you are the gardener
and the lotus flower
of your own body.

144

you flood
my mind everyday
wrapped in words
like the morning's
newspaper

with nothing new to say,
only different ways
to tell them.

146

when you left,
you took the cages
we had built around
each other's secrets

i cower alone at night
afraid of the wild things
you've released inside of me

148

i am wild
i am wild again
this is what
your leaving
did to me.

150

i am
your
lingering
scent.

152

my palm was caked with
crushed flowers and dirt
the first day your hand took mine
but you were faithful and patient,
you understood that i still had things
i couldn't let go of just yet
and with your fingers laced through mine,
you helped me open up

you loved me honestly.

as i sifted through the flowers worth keeping,
you never let my hand go,

you caught all of my fallen dirt,
and you blew it to the wind.

154

i wish in one direction
but look in the other,
for nothing i have ever wanted
has come out the way i expected.

unfold my soul
and you will find your name
written
on every petal

158

i don't want my past
to be my story.

i want to give the pen
to the person i became in spite of it,
for i am not a tragedy
full of sympathetic words,
i am the continuing tale
of a warrior who made it back home
because the past
never made it
to my next chapter.

160

bury your past.
let flowers grow
where you lay.

162

the present is a seed
planted by the past

it takes the careful
watering of the future
for it to blossom into something beautiful.

164

your roots
are buried
deep within you.

sometimes you
have to dig through
all the dirt to know
what kind of flower
you truly are.

166

my mother used to tell me
to surround myself with beauty
no matter how ugly the world may seem.

be a lotus, she'd say.
a lotus may grow on filth,
but it's the rain that keeps her clean.

never rush to unfold
the contents of your heart.

you are a strange flower
in bloom,
don't let them pick and name you
before you have
the chance to blossom.

170

it's an hour before sunrise in india right now
and the chai wallahs have begun
releasing spiced coils of smoke
into the air to rouse the city.
the fishermen
have already disappeared into the fog of the sea,
they drift in silence as they listen to the prayers
echoing from the temples ashore.
around the river,
the birds form the sickle moon of an elephant's tusk,
chiming songs as sweet as the bells of a royal wedding.

they say there is a special energy in the air
the hours before the sun rises,
the breeze enters the body as a spark
and carries us throughout the day.

right now it's late afternoon
and we're in bed,
our palms against the sun
as we filter slivers of dying light
across the sheets.

i'm told that in india,
people do more before the sunrise
than we do in an entire day,
but i'm afraid that this morning
everyone will have to wait,

because the sun hasn't left our room yet,
we've got her trapped between our palms
as sparks dance inside the space
between your mouth, and mine.

172

there will always be
someone who suffers
more than you,
but does the sky
need a reason to weep?

we are, after all,
made of the same air,
moon and stars.

174

like a lotus
bathed in dirt,
some people
are drenched
in pain,
but you could
never tell
by the way
they blossom.

176

seek forgiveness in yourself before searching for it in others,
people will pick and choose the parts of you they love
before discarding the rest.

but darling,
you are not a backyard full of weeds
needing to be pulled,
you are a garden of roses aching with thorns.

you deserve to be loved
only by someone
who knows how to hold all of you.

178

love doesn't wait
for you to get better,
it doesn't travel
down familiar roads,
and it doesn't always
show up in the skin
of another person.

sometimes love
is the steps you take
to keep getting out of bed.

sometimes love
is walking down new roads
even if every step
is more painful than the last.

sometimes love
is making it back home
looking at yourself in the mirror,
and simply being happy
that you're still alive.

my wounds
don't feel
like wounds
in your hands.
they feel
like beginnings,
like a chance
to make things
right again.

182

our souls
have been waiting
lifetimes
for our hearts
to finally meet.

your soul is attracted
to people the way
flowers are attracted
to the sun.
surround yourself
only with those who
want to see you grow.

seek the world
and you will only
lose yourself.

seek yourself
and you will
discover the world.

if i knew then
what i know now,
i wouldn't change
a single thing.

i have grown into
a better person
because of you,
and that's something
you can never
take back.

love isn't where
we hide our ghosts.
love is where
we release them.

192

people are scars,
some are meant
to be in our lives
for a brief
amount of time.

some
are meant
to last forever.

when you create
something from
your soul,
it shows.

mountains move,
you can feel them
shiver within you.

196

you are a poem
the earth wrote
to keep me
a part of it.

198

if giving leaves you
feeling empty
you're giving too much
to the wrong person.

200

we are
what
could
have
been.

you
and i,

we are
an entire
universe.

202

you were planted
in this world
to blossom many times,
you were meant to lose
and find love again.

there are flowers
in this world we will
never see again

perhaps people
are not so different.

we put our hearts
into what we love.
we stain it with
our own blood.

206

i no longer wish for shelter
from the storm
but for the calm of the sea
to overcome it.

208

continents drift

so do people

this is how
we make new homes.

210

my heart has been split
like the oceans of the world,

each one longs for you.

212

you, the origin of my love.
you, my homeland.

healing is an art,
it takes time.
it takes practice.
it takes love.

216

i want to write a story about the last day
we spent together. i want to write about the
river we sat beside and the indian film songs
we sang while balancing on rocks slippery
with moss, how we devoured melted cadburys
with the berries we picked as we chased a golden
chain of sunlight draped around the river bank.

i want to write chapters on our memories
but somehow,
stories never feel complete

so instead,
i'll write you a poem.

i sat near that river bank the day after you died
watching the water flow over the naked rocks
now stripped of moss, and finally,
i understood.

wherever the water flows,
something always leaves with it.

the pain,
it will leave
once it has finished
teaching you.

the day my parents were divorced
i sat waiting in front of the television
absorbed in a documentary about swans

swans mate for life,
a distant voice narrated in my head
and they will remain in pairs until the very end.

i watched, enthralled at how these swans
never ventured far from one another.

my father came out first,
he gave me a hug and sat with me for a while
never saying a word.
i looked back at the screen
just in time to see the two swans spread their wings
and fly straight into the sun,
two silver jets chalking the brilliant sky.

when i looked back up,
he was gone.

222

listen to your blood.
go where it beats.

224

escape doesn't always
mean running away

sometimes escape
is simply
making it back home

i woke up this morning
to tell you the sun has risen,
to say that the mornings
are still in bloom like fire
lilies carpeting a burnt sky

i woke up this morning
to tell you the yellow headed
blackbirds have decorated
the pinetree outside again
and when they dance,
the leaves turn into the eyelets
of a large peacock tail
spread just for us

i woke up this morning
to say that my heart still
feels empty but my soul
complete like the full moon
in a cloudless sky

that nothing has changed
since you've been gone,
that the sun still rises
and the trees still spread
their wings and that my heart
is still full of stars

i woke up this morning
to tell you i am healing,
that with every burnt sky
a new flower grows in its
place, petal by petal,

to tell you that i am full
of a song i still don't know
the words to yet but
it is coming,
and one day
i will sing it for you.

228

may roses blossom from your pain